THE BIBLE LANDS HOLYLAND JOURNEY

385 Photographs

Editor: Reuven Dorot

Written by: Dr.Randall D. Smith

Book Designed by: Gal Kaldcron

Cover Design By: Novelty Ltd

Photographers:

Itamar Grinberg, Zev Radovan, Duby Tal, Moni Haramati/Albatross, ASAP/ Garo Nalbandian,

Lev Borodulin, Hanan Isachar, Israel Talby, Nitsan Shorer, Bouky Boaz, Eitan Simanor, Richard Nowitz, David Harris,

Avi Hirschfield, Eyal Bartov, Joel Fishman, ASAP

Consultant: Larry S. Price, Map: Alex Firley

Published by: DOKO

Special thanks to: Israel Antiquities Authorities, The Israel Museum

DOKO is a leading production and distribution company of biblical and historical media products.
We publish videos, books, CD ROM, and compact discs.
For a free catalogue of our product line please write to: DOKO

Distributed by:
DOKO Entertainment (1996) Ltd. 10 Ha' Amal St. P.O. Box 611, Or Yudea 60371 Israel
bible@biblelandshop.com   www.biblelandshop.net
Tel. 972-3-634-4776 Fax: 972-3-634-4690

MAP OF ISRAEL

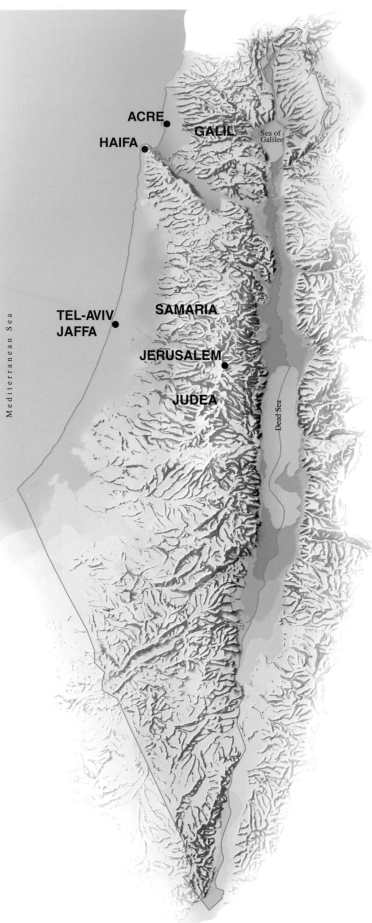

ACRE

HAIFA

GALIL

Sea of Galilee

TEL-AVIV
JAFFA

SAMARIA

JERUSALEM

JUDEA

Mediterranean Sea

Dead Sea

Attempting to capture the essence of the Holy Land has been an incredible challenge. We have tried to show the land in all its color and diversity. First, we wanted to tell the story of Jesus' life by showing the places where events are recalled from His ministry. Second, we wanted to show the incredible contrasts and beauty of the landscape, Finally, we wanted to help visitors recall the important facts about each site.

This book is not in geographical order, but rather follows the basic accepted chronology of the life of Jesus. In order to make the logic of the sites clearer, we have imposed the life of Jesus over the table of contents (page 3) for easy reference. We have also included many popular places that having nothing to do with the life of Jesus but which were simply nearby the sites of the Jesus story. In this way we were able to include Akko, Haifa and the other interesting places which give a more accurate picture of what a visit to this land entails.

Many sites include a time line which puts a date on the most important structure built on the site. Small symbols identify which religious groups (Jewish, Christian, Moslem) hold the place sacred or remember significant events there. We have included meaningful sites for Christians of different traditions, and included all of the popular sites from the gospels.

Several maps of the "land of Jesus" were created to make the story easier to follow (pp. 30, 78). In order to make this an easy reference source for those touring the land, the beginning of the book includes a brief historical chart, while a list of the Bible passages for each site is placed at the end. This book is made up of new photographs taken just for this work. Many show the changes to the holy sites, including recent renovations at places like the Holy Sepulchre and St. Peter en Gallicantu.

We believe that this book is a special blend of the story of the ministry of our Lord mixed with the sites that recall His work. This theme, interwoven with other locations from the land of the Bible, adds a rich, new understanding to the meaning of the work of Jesus of Nazareth. We trust it will also bring back many pleasant memories for those who visited the lands of the Bible.

Dr. Randall D. Smith, Director
Christian Travel Study Programs
Jerusalem

TABLE OF CONTENTS

Nazareth

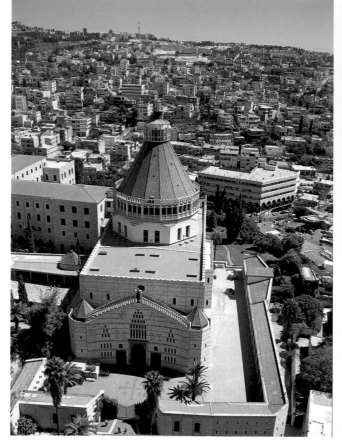

Once a small village in the Galilee with "nothing good" (see Jn. 1:46), the bustling city of Nazareth today boasts the largest Arab Christian population in the Holy Land. One of the city's highlights is the "Basilica of the Annunciation", a church which reminds worshipers that the angel Gabriel announced to the virgin Mary she would bear the Messiah (Luke 1).

MADONNA DELLE LACRIME DI SIRACUSA

The Basilica's outer design recalls the Aramaic meaning of Nazareth, a watchtower (p.4, left). It is built over carefully excavated ancient Nazareth homes (p. 4, upper right) which are today open to visitors.
The interior of the Basilica (above) contains ruins of two earlier churches, all built against an ancient house that tradition says is the site of the angelic announcement. The modern church was constructed in 1968 and contains colorful artwork depicting "Madonna and Child" from many countries.

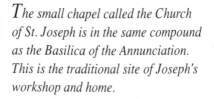

The small chapel called the Church of St. Joseph is in the same compound as the Basilica of the Annunciation. This is the traditional site of Joseph's workshop and home.

The area contains what appears to be a ritual bath (left) perhaps used by an early Jewish Christian community.

The Church of St. Joseph (right) was built in 1914 over caves which may have been silos, cisterns or the lower rooms of ancient houses.

The excavations show that Nazareth was a poor village which probably had less than four hundred people when Jesus lived here as a boy.

Nazareth: Mary's Well

In addition to the Basilica of the Annunciation, Nazareth contains other sites which remind worshipers of important events in the life of Jesus.

About 300 meters north of the Basilica is the Greek Orthodox Church of St. Gabriel (p.6, lower). Built in 1781 over the ruins of a Twelfth Century Crusader church, St. Gabriel's stands above a source of the ancient spring which feeds the "Virgin's Fountain" (lower left), where many Orthodox Christians believe the annunciation took place.

When Jesus returned to Nazareth to preach in his home town, the reception in the local synagogue was hostile (Lk. 4). Today this is recalled in the Greek Catholic "Synagogue Church" (center).

Ein Karem

Following the annunciation in Nazareth, the Gospel according to St. Luke records that Mary went to a village in the hill country of Judea to visit with Elizabeth for three months (Lk. 1).

The place is now remembered as Ein Karem.

The Church of the Visitation is built above a cave that, according to a fifth century tradition, was near the meeting place of Mary and Elizabeth.

Both women were with child, and the baby leaped within Elizabeth when Mary came into the house (Lk. 1:44).

Inside the church 41 different plaques, each in a different language, bear the words of Mary to Elizabeth. Named "The Magnificat," Mary's celebrated words are recorded in the Gospel, "My soul magnifies the Lord, and my spirit rejoices in God my Savior" (Lk. 1:46ff).

This exquisite structure, which helps fill this quaint village with the sound of church bells each day, has been maintained by the Franciscans since it was constructed in 1938.

Bethlehem: The Church of the Nativity

From the village of Bethlehem on the edge of the Judean Desert, the visitor gazes upon the stark mountains of Moab (above). Even with only about 40,000 residents today, Bethlehem is still world famous because of its importance in several Bible stories.

First mentioned in the Book of Ruth, Bethlehem means the "house of Bread" in Hebrew. This was the town which drew Naomi back after a famine had caused her to flee (Ruth 3), but it was the stories of two different kings which engraved its name in history. The first story began when King David was brought before Samuel the prophet and anointed with oil. (1 Ki. 16). Later, another king - the Messiah - was to come from Bethlehem.

The prophet Micah promised, "But you Bethlehem, Ephrata, out of you shall He come forth." (Mic. 5:2). Centuries later, Herod the Great asked, "Where will the Messiah be born?" The scholars of his day replied, "Bethlehem" (Mt. 2:5). Today, the Church of the Nativity, with its small doorway (right) marks a place to remember the birth of Jesus. Thousands come each year to celebrate the nativity in this town (p.11).

329

*T*he church of the nativity is built above a cave which may have been the place of Jesus' nativity. After the time of Jesus, the cave was apparently covered by a pagan shrine to Adonis built by Emperor Hadrian in 135 CE. This shrine was torn down by Queen Helena, who erected the first Church of the Nativity in 329.

From the dedication of that church in May of 339 until St. Jerome moved there in 384, little had changed of the large octagonal church except the mosaic tiles on the floor, which were added around 390 and can still be seen today. Damaged by an uprising of the Samaritans in 522, the church was entirely renovated by Emperor Justinian in 527. Because of a mosaic of the Magi dressed in Persian garb, when the Persians rampaged through the land in 614 destroying churches, they left this church alone.

The Crusaders rennovated the church, adding artistic touches, and then used it as the coronation place of Baldwin I, who was crowned King of the Latin Kingdom on Christmas Day 1100 CE. The place of the nativity is celebrated in the cave beneath the altar.

The cave includes two small lobes, one with a star (p. 13, bottom) to mark the place of Jesus' birth, the other to mark the place of the manger and the repose of the holy family. (p.13, top)

Bethlehem: Church of St. Catherine

Bethlehem: The Milk Grotto

*A*nother church in Bethlehem is the Church of St. Catherine (p. 14), the Latin Catholic Church for the Nativity festival. Dedicated to the martyr St. Catherine, the wheel like lamps recall her death.

*B*eneath the main sanctuary are three caves, two of them house the "Chapel of St. Jerome", who lived in these caves when he translated the Old and New Testaments into Latin (The Vulgate). The adjacent "Chapel of the Innocents" recalls the terror of Herod the Great, who ordered the male children of Bethlehem to be slaughtered (Mt. 2:13-18).

*N*earby, the small but ornate chapel of the Milk Grotto (above) is dedicated to the nurturing of the baby Jesus by Mary.

A famous statue of the holy family (left) fleeing to Egypt reminds pilgrims of the escape from Herod's tyranny (Mt. 2:14).

The Shepherd's Fields

On the edge of Bethlehem are fields that are used for grazing land for the sheep and goats common to this area (below). Three places of worship recall the story of the shepherds that witnessed the multitude of angels proclaiming Messiah's birth (Luke 2).

Herodion

Though Herod was in Jerusalem when the Magi visited him (Mt. 2), he also had this palace, closer to Bethlehem. This palace fortress resembles a volcano. It was surrounded by a man made mountain adorned with an exterior white marble staircase. Inside were a royal apartment and ceremonial halls. Herod is said to be buried within the mountain.

-24

Village Life

In the south of the country, the winter wheat is first cut with a sickle (center) and then crushed on a threshing floor (left, bottom) before the wheat is separated from the chaff (see Lk.3:17) with the use of a winnowing fork (right). Another important crop is the olive. After the harvest, olives are place under the weight of a crushing stone (below) to squeeze out the precious oil.

For generations, the people of the Holy Land have depended on the land for their living. Long ago God promised, "The land which I give you will be a land flowing with milk and honey.".

*T*hough modern equipment is available in the country, many families prefer the traditional ways of harvesting.

The olive press (left) uses the weight of the stones to pull down the beam and squeeze the bags of crushed olives near the fulcrum. Beyond the grain and olive harvests, the land yields a grape harvest and an important citrus crop.

The Tomb of Rachel

*R*achel died in childbirth on the way to Bethlehem (Gen. 35:16-20). Though 1 Samuel 10:2 seems to suggest that the tomb was north of Jerusalem, for generations it has been remembered here, near Bethlehem.

Today, this fifteenth century building has become a place of pilgrimage for Jews, Christians and Moslems. Women come here to pray for fertility and for healthy children. The Gospel of St. Matthew records in the Nativity story that Herod's slaughtering of the children was from a prophecy of Jeremiah the prophet that Rachel was "weeping for her children because they were no more." (Jer. 31:15; Mt. 2:18)

-1900

Solomon's Pools

*S*outh of Bethlehem are three beautiful ancient water reservoirs known as Solomon's pools. Probably built by Herod the Great, the pools collected water from the surrounding hills and stored it until needed in Jerusalem.

Stretching for miles, the aqueduct and pipeline system that brought water to the capital city has been uncovered in a number of places along the Bethlehem-Jerusalem highway.

-30

Hebron

*T*he landscape of the city of Hebron is still dominated by the tombs of the Patriarchs and Matriarchs (above). Here Abraham purchased burial caves for his family (Gen. 23).

Much later a large building above the caves was built to honor Abraham, Sarah, Isaac, Rebekkah, Leah and Jacob. The interior (right) has been a place of prayer for centuries for both Moslems and Jews.

Ophel Excavations

*T*he Ophel ridge is filled with excavations that help to paint a clearer picture of the magnificent Temple, whose ruins are still being uncovered by archaeologists (below). Baths near the stairway (right), called "mikvaot" were used in cleansing rituals practiced before entering the Temple, just as Mary did after giving birth to Jesus (Lk. 2:22ff).

Mammoth construction stones found below the pinnacle of the Temple (below) have helped in reconstructing models (right, above) of the area. The area is mentioned in the testing of Jesus (Mt. 4). A stairway to the south porch has also been uncovered (below).

The Western Wall

*T*he Temple was the heart of the Jewish world until its destruction in 70 CE by theRoman general Titus.

The central place for the celebrations of Judaism, Mary took the baby Jesus there as a religious duty, to be presented in the Temple's courts (Ex. 13:2).

During this presentation an old man named Simeon, and later the prophetess Anna, foretold the future greatness of the child (Lk 2:22-38).

Today the area surrounding the Western Wall is once again alive with prayer and the study of the Torah scrolls, as the Temple had been so long ago. No longer the "Wailing Wall", it is now a place of holy celebration.

The joyous coming of age ceremony of the "Bar Mitzvah" is a weekly event at the wall (below).

*T*he Western Wall, the holiest place of prayer for Jews today, is all that remains of the massive western porch that once surrounded the Temple, built by Herod the Great.

70

The Journey to Egypt

The hearts of Jewish people were not only tied to the Temple in Jerusalem, but also to the memory of the southern deserts, and to the famous journey of the Exodus. Moses lead them through the "great and terrible wilderness", to the mountain of the law (Ex. 20). The wilderness played a role in the lives of Elijah (1 Ki . 19), and of John the Baptist (Lk.1:80), and became part of the life of Jesus.

Only the Gospel according to St. Matthew (Mt. 2:13-18) records the journey of Joseph, Mary and the baby Jesus into Egypt, and recalls the prophecy, "Out of Egypt have I called my Son" (Hosea 11:1).

-5-4

Avdat

*T*rading stations and settlements like that at Avdat were discovered along the ancient caravan routes that crossed the deserts. Founded more than 2000 years ago, the village of Avdat was located along the caravan route that ran from the east along the Dead Sea to Egypt.

Though an abandoned ruin today, the surrounding fields once produced a rich grape crop which was irrigated by tiny amounts of rainfall ingeniously channeled into the vineyards. Many of the present ruins come from the later Byzantine settlement (Sixth Century).

550

Mount Sinai (Egypt)

*T*he rugged mountains of the Sinai are surrounded by sandy beaches and the beautiful blue waters of the Red Sea. (above)

Though the location of Mt Sinai is uncertain, Jebel Musa (left) stands in the mountain ranges of the Sinai peninsula, and since at least the sixth century CE has been visited by pilgrims who considered it a possible site for the mountain of the Law (Ex. 19-20). Below the precipice (p.27) of Jebel Musa is the Greek Orthodox monastery of Santa Catherina, named after the fourth century Christian martyr St. Catherine of Alexandria, whose bones are said to have been placed nearby.

The monastery houses an ancient manuscript library and icons from the early periods of the Christian faith.

380

Desert Life and the Bedouin

*S*ince the time of Abraham, the dry lands to the south have been inhabited by nomadic tribes. Today, these Bedouin tribes are Moslem Arabs who continue to preserve an ancient way of life. Shepherds who constantly flow back and forth across the borders of the Near East states, they are driven from place to place in search of new grazing land for their sheep and goats. Using wool to weave tents and rugs (below), they trade their handi-crafts for goods at the village markets. In some areas there is enough rainfall for a brief winter wheat harvest, supplying grains for daily bread.

Preserving their culture in music, hand-made instruments accompany the evening's hospitality in the tents. A proud heritage is preserved in the story-telling that accompanies the grinding and serving of coffee. Many of the stories, passed down for generations, teach the children lessons of honor and happiness.

Traveling in the Land of Jesus

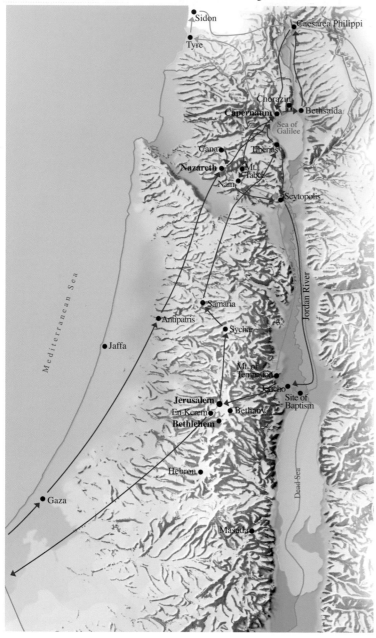

After the death of Herod the Great, the Gospel of St. Matthew records the story of the return of Joseph, Mary and Jesus to Nazareth (Mt. 2:19-23). The exact path of this journey to Nazareth is unclear, but much is known about the trade routes and main roads of that time.

The major international coastal highway was called the "Via Maris", which passed through the Galilee region on its way from Egypt to Syria. A roadway popular with religiously observant Jews ran from Jerusalem through Perea and Decapolis to the Galilee, avoiding the center of the country where the ill-regarded Samaritans lived.

To attend the Temple's main religious festivals - like Succoth (Tabernacles), Pesach (Passover), or Shavuoth (Pentecost) - many Jews of the Galilee would use the Perean road. Late in the ministry of Jesus, he remained in Perea teaching for as many as six months (Lk. 10-19).

On a journey to the Temple when Jesus was about twelve years of age (Lk. 2:41-50) the gospel records that Jesus' parents lost Him for three days. After a search, they found Him in the Temple discussing the Law of Moses with the rabbis. When confronted by His relieved parents, Jesus said, "Did you not know I would be about my Father's business?" The model below illustrates the huge Temple area that the worried parents searched.

→ Flight to Egipt and return to Nazareth

→ Baptism and sojourn in the desert

→ Galilean journeys and to Caesarea Philippi

→ Journey to Tyre and Sidon

→ Journey to and from Jerusalem

The Jordan River

Journeys to Jerusalem usually went through the Jordan Valley, on a path alongside the Jordan River. The river flows from four streams that appear along the slopes of Mt. Hermon, each a result of the melting snowfalls from the peaks above.

From its sources, like at the Banias stream (above) the water flows down to the Sea of Galilee. As the river tumbles southward, whitewater areas (below) make rafting and kayaking an exciting and chilling excursion.

The river flows a distance of only 65 miles as the crow flies, from its sources to the river's end at the Dead Sea. From overhead the river looks like a snake, winding and curving , stretching the short distance to over 160 miles.

Though small in size, the Jordan plays a role in many Biblical stories, including the crossing of the river by the Israelites with Joshua (Joshua 3), the miraculous floating of the axe head (2 Kings 6), the healing of Naaman of leprosy by washing in the river (2 Kings 5), and the baptism of Jesus (Mt. 3).

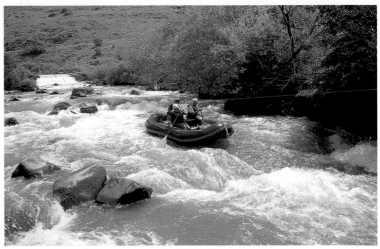

Yardenit

*A*ll four gospels start the public ministry of Jesus with His baptism by John in the Jordan River (Mt. 3, Mk. 1, Lk. 3, Jn. 1).

The ministry of John included preaching repentance toward God, and calling for a symbolic cleansing in the river.

Jesus attended one such gathering and asked John to baptize Him in the water.

Later, Jesus commanded His followers to observe baptism (Mt 28:19-20).

1981

The Monastery of St. Jerasimos

*M*any pilgrims are baptized in the Jordan River today. Though some choose the newer site built for this purpose (p.32) at Yardenit, the traditional site of the Greek Orthodox is still visited once each year (below).

The Monastery of St. Jerasimos is maintained by the Orthodox Church , as is the steep bank behind it which marks the traditional area for the ministry of John the Baptist. This monastery is one of twenty founded in the Judean Wilderness during the Byzantine period.

Qumran

Though the family of John the Baptist was from the hill country of Judea (Lk. 1:39-40), John grew up in the "desert" of Judea (Lk.1:80). Because he was the child of elderly parents, some scholars speculate that he may have been adopted by a sect in a desert monastery, like the one found here at Qumran.

The discovery of the Dead Sea Scrolls in caves nearby encouraged archaeologists to restore Qumran, the site that housed a monastery of ancient scroll copyists. Twenty-five miles southeast of Jerusalem (40 km.), Qumran is near the salty Dead Sea, and may be the Biblical site of the "city of Salt" (Josh. 15). Not far away, John began his baptizing ministry.

The Shrine of the Book

Some of the Dead Sea Scrolls found in the Qumran area are now on display in an unusually shaped building in the Israel museum in Jerusalem called The Shrine of the Book.

The white dome on the exterior of the museum (above) is shaped to resemble the ancient storage jars of the scrolls. The white color is contrasted against the black wall behind the dome, designed to remind visitors of the important scroll named, "The war of the sons of light and the sons of darkness".

Since the discovery of the scrolls in the Dead Sea caves in 1947, much research has been done to examine the contents of the collection. The scrolls have every book of the Hebrew Bible (with the possible exception of Esther), along with a number of other documents from that Qumran community.

Inside the museum (right), a replica of the famous "Isaiah scroll" is positioned on a wooden rod to look like a scroll from a synagogue.

Jericho

Also near the Dead Sea, Jericho is both the oldest known walled city on earth (8000 BCE) and the world's lowest city, (1200 feet below sea level).

With a spring that releases 1000 gallons of water per minute, this oasis has been called the "City of a Thousand Palms".

An archaeological dig in the 1960's (center, left) uncovered an ancient city tower dating back to about 7000 BCE, and interesting artifacts (left) of the city's inhabitants.

In the Bible, the city was conquered by Joshua (Josh. 2), but left as rubble for most of the Old Testament (1 Ki. 16:34). Herod the Great built a winter palace not far from the old ruins, causing a new city to sprout on the plain nearby.

Zacchaeus, the short tax collector who climbed the tree to see Jesus pass by, was a resident of the new city (Lk 19:1ff) along with the blind Bartimeaus, who was healed by Jesus (Mk. 10:46ff).

Hisham's Palace

On the northern edge of Jericho stands the remains of a building commonly called "Hisham's Palace", because at first archaelogists thought it was built by the Arab ruler Hisham (724-743 CE).

Later, scholars decided it was probably built by his nephew, whose one-year rule ended with his assassination. The site has beautiful mosaic floors, a bath complex, and a palace - all unfinished.

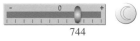

744

The Monastery of the Temptation

*T*he gospels describe the forty day fast and testing experience of Jesus in the Wilderness of Judea (Mt. 4:1-11) after the baptism in the Jordan by John. The actual location of the temptation is not known, but the first and third temptations are remembered at the monastery on Jebel Quarantel, or "the mountain of the forty".

Two sites were built in the twelfth century to recall the story, one in a cave on the side of the cliff, and one at the summit. These buildings were in ruins by the time a pilgrim visited in the fourteenth century. The cliff side monastery was restored around 1900. Today, there is an interior cave chapel to remind pilgrims of the fasting of Jesus, when He refused to turn the stones into bread.

1180

The Mar Saba Monastery

*M*ar Saba, with its blue domes and red tiled roof, is a striking example of the many monastic communities which have made the Wilderness of Judea their home over the centuries. This monastery was founded by St. Sabas in 482 CE, and survived a savage attack by the Persians in 614, when many of the monks were martyred. Remains of the Persian's savagery can still be seen inside the monastery.

The "golden age" of Mar Saba was in the eighth century, when the monastery housed a number of important scholars. One was St. John Damascene, whose compelling arguments defending the use of images in religious places later allowed the discovery of many Renaissance church artists. This entire monastery was restored after an earthquake in 1834.

Cana

*F*ollowing the temptation in the wilderness, Jesus travelled with His first five disciples (Jn. 1) to a wedding in the Galilee village of Cana.

A church now stands in the village of Kfar Kana with jars (below) to remind visitors of the story of Jesus' first miracle, turning water into wine (Jn. 2).

Though the location of ancient Cana is disputed, this church is built above ancient ruins, including an earlier Christian worship site.

1879

*T*he New Testament mentions Cana three times: - the wedding miracle (Jn. 2); the healing of the Capernaum official's son (Jn. 4:46-54); and the village of Nathaniel's family - the disciple of the Lord (John 21).

Megiddo

*M*any sites in the Galilee attract visitors to the land of the Bible. A popular archaeological restoration is that of Megiddo. Strategically located on the ancient Via Maris highway (Way of the Sea), Megiddo has a history that spans more than 3500 years.

Destroyed and rebuilt more than 20 times on the same spot, this ruin creates a flat plateau some sixty feet above the level of the surrounding plain. Visitors can walk through a gate dating back to the masons of King Solomon (1 Kings 9:15), and a water system cut through solid rock around the time of King Ahab (right).

Haifa

The coastline of Israel has a mountain range called Mt. Carmel, or "the vineyard of the Lord," that pushes out to the Mediterranean Sea.
The modern city of Haifa now stretches along the northern face of the mountain from the edge of the Mediterranean to the summit of Carmel.
Established in the 1930's, Haifa is today Israel's third largest city, and home to the country's most important heavy industry port.
The central landmark of the city is the world center of the Bahai faith with its beautifully glittering gold dome. The Bahai came from Persia around 1844 and now have more than two million followers, with Haifa as their holy city.

1930

Acre

Acre (also Akko) is a 4000 year old port that was promised to the tribe of Asher (Jud. 1:31) When St. Paul visited the city it was called by its Greek name, Ptolemais (Acts 21:7). The Khan el-Umdan (left, below) or "Inn of the Columns" was erected in 1906 by the Ottoman Sultan Abdul Hamid.

The inn's clock tower helps define the skyline of today's Akko. The Al Jazzar mosque (right), built in 1781, is named after the "butcher of Akko" who successfully held off Napolean's army by threatening to execute any soldier who retreated.

Rosh Hanikra

Rosh Hanikra is a naturally beautiful place, and a popular destination for visitors to the Holy Land. Tucked in below the border crossing into Lebanon, the pounding surf carved out a white cliff terrace that glows in the late afternoon sun.

Beth Shearim

170

*N*orthwest of the Jezreel valley, Beth Shearim, or "house of gates," is all that remains of an ancient village.
31 catacombs filled with stone coffins were found in nearby caves. Some coffins were adorned with Jewish symbols like the menorah. Two coffins were inscribed with the names of Rabbi Judah the prince's two sons, Shimon and Gamaliel.

Sepphorus (Zippori)

*T*he once beautiful city of Sepphorus, although not mentioned in the gospels, was under reconstruction when Jesus was growing up in Nazareth just six miles away. Some Christian traditions relate that the family of Mary, Jesus' mother, was from Zippori.

The city was founded in the second century BCE, and was taken by Herod the Great in 37 BCE when he attacked during a snowstorm. After his death, the city rioted in protest to Roman occupation and was destroyed.

Herod Antipas rebuilt the city. Later, the city became especially important after the Sanhedrin moved here, and under the skilled hands of Judah HaNasi compiled the Mishnah, a collection of Hebrew oral law.

Capernaum: The Greek Orthodox Chapel

After choosing His first disciples, and paying a brief visit near Cana, Jesus moved to the seaside town of Capernaum, where He began His first ministry (Mt. 4:12). The tranquil setting of this Chapel at Capernaum allows Christians from the Orthodox tradition to reflect on the event. The modern brightly domed structure was built amid the 7th century CE ruins of the Capernaum fishing village. These ruins were once well constructed buildings. Also found here were 800 year old rooms with indoor pools, which may have been a fish market of that period.

Capernaum: The House of St. Peter

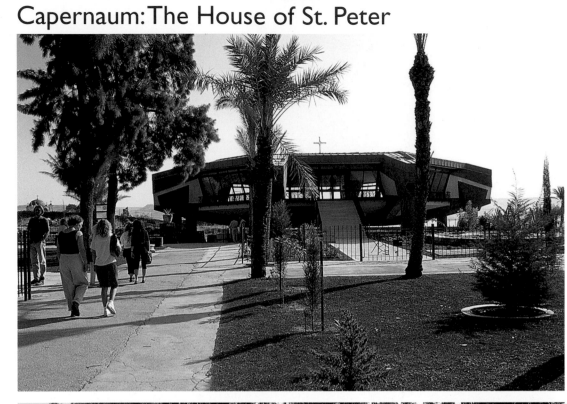

The ancient city of Capernaum was where many of the recorded miracles and teachings of Jesus (Mk. 1; 4) took place. Many believe the healing of St. Peter's mother in law (Mk.1:29ff) happened here, (below), and the site is marked by a new church (left) recently built above it.

Capernaum: The Synagogue

The city of Capernaum, which is now thought to have contained between 4000 and 5000 people in the time of Jesus, was referred to as His "home town" because He was so often there (Mt.:1; Mk. 2:1.)

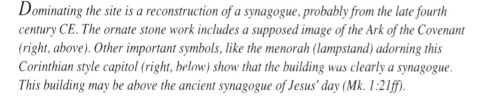

Dominating the site is a reconstruction of a synagogue, probably from the late fourth century CE. The ornate stone work includes a supposed image of the Ark of the Covenant (right, above). Other important symbols, like the menorah (lampstand) adorning this Corinthian style capitol (right, below) show that the building was clearly a synagogue. This building may be above the ancient synagogue of Jesus' day (Mk. 1:21ff).

Archaeologists have uncovered houses built around irregular courtyards in the "insulus" style, where the rooms hug the outer wall of the property like 'insulation'. Each home provided living space for the entire extended family.

*T*he main harbor of the Sea of Galilee is in the city of Tiberias (p.50, above). Fresh water springs from the slopes of Mt. Hermon in the north flow into the Jordan River which then fills the lake.

The Sea is about 8 miles wide and 13 miles long. Its Hebrew name, Kinneret, comes from the word for harp, which is the shape of the sea. In the Gospels it is called by various names: Gennesaret (Lk.8) from the name of a nearby Canaanite city, and the Sea of Tiberias (Jn. 6; 21). The view from Mt. Arbel (p. 50, lower) shows the vast plain of Gennesaret, where it was recorded many of Jesus' works were performed.

Boats still fish in these water (above). A recent discovery of an ancient fishing craft (left), dated between 100 BCE and 100 CE, shows marine construction techniques used in the time of Jesus. This boat was found buried in clay at the Sea's edge. It can now be seen in a museum north of ancient Magdala.

-100

The landscape along the shore of the Sea of Galilee was the backdrop for a number of events recorded in the ministry of Jesus - healing, performing miracles, and teaching. Church history mentions places like Tabgha as one of the many early sites of these episodes. An abbreviated form of the Greek name of this site is 'Heptapagon', or "the place of seven springs." At Tabgha two churches remember the teaching, and miraculous ministry of Jesus. Also on the site are the ruins of a chapel that once recalled the "Sermon on the Mount". The most prominent church recalls the feeding of the thousands (Jn.6) from the "five loaves and two fishes".

The halls of the Church of the Multiplication were recently restored over the exact lines of the fifth century chapel that once stood there (left).

The ancient mosaics have been incorporated into the new floor. Nearby is the black basalt stone chapel on the edge of the sea called the "Chapel of the Primacy" (p.52.) Built in 1933, the small interior (top left) recalls the discussion the resurrected Christ had with His disciple, Peter (Jn. 21).

On a summit overlooking the Sea of Galilee, the Franciscans built a domed octagonal church to remind pilgrims of the setting of the eight beatitudes of Jesus recorded in the "Sermon on the Mount" (Mt. 5-7). Built in the 1930's, the church is set in one of the most beautiful gardens in the land.

The interior of the church includes a glittering gold dome, an ornate altar, and eight stained glass windows with the beatitudes written on them.

The church was designed by the famous Italian architect Antonio Barluzzi, who profoundly influenced modern church art and architecture in the Holy Land. The design of the long windows and colonnaded porch offers the pilgrim a view the surrounding hillsides.

This was the backdrop for the sayings of Jesus in the Gospels.

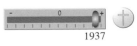

1937

Chorazin

*M*any works of Jesus took place in Chorazin. Its inhabitants were condemned by Jesus for their disbelief (Mt. 11). At its ancient synagogue archaeologists found the "seat of Moses" (Mt. 23:2), the inscribed carved stone bench of a local teacher.

370

Hammat Tiberias

*I*n the gospel accounts, in addition to His teaching ministry, Jesus often healed the sick (Mk. 2:1-12; Lk. 5:6ff). Many of the afflicted gathered near the Sea of Galilee to use the healing centers that developed near the hot springs.

One such center was at Hammat Tiberias, where the medicinal baths were used as early as the first century. Even then the waters were a constant 60 degrees centigrade (140 F). A later synagogue found at the site (fourth century) had a floor (left) that mixed Jewish religious symbols with the twelve signs of the zodiac.

375

Kursi

470

Jesus normally ministered in the religious Jewish areas northwest of the Sea of Galilee, but several times He crossed the sea to the Gentile territories on the east side (Mk. 4:35; 6:45ff). During one trip, the gospels record that an exorcism of demons into swine took place (Mark 5:1ff). Byzantine Christians recalled the event in the monastery at Kursi.

Hammat Gader

In the fourth century, the hot baths at Hammat Gader (below) were among the best in the Roman world. Centuries later they still draw visitors. The nearby alligator park is a popular attraction.

380

Gamala

Gamala (from "camel") was a Zealot city near the Sea of Galilee that was encircled by the Romans in 67 CE. Thousands fell fighting the Romans. When the 5,000 remaining Zealots saw that they could not win, they leaped to their deaths rather than become Roman slaves.

A synagogue (right) from the period before the Temple's destruction was uncovered on the site. Though we have no record of Jesus ministering at Gamala, we do know that at least one of his followers, Simon, had once been a Zealot.

Mt. Hermon and the Huleh Valley

During a trip away from the Sea with His disciples, Jesus took them to a high mountain apart (Mt. 17; Mk. 8). Mt Hermon is the highest mountain in the Near East (9200 feet ASL). Its snows provide the only skiing around, as well as one third of the country's drinking water. Below the mountain are the drained swamps of the Huleh valley.

Banias

At the foot of Mt. Hermon, north of the Sea of Galilee, the spring of Banias flows from the ground south to the Jordan river. Once named Paneas in Greek, the cave was dedicated to the mythical shepherd god, Pan. Later, the region of this Greek city fell under the control of Herod Philip, and was renamed Caesarea Phillipi.

Withdrawing from the crowds with His disciples, Jesus came to the region outside the city to ask them the critical question, "Who do you say that I am?" (Matthew 16:13).

Recent excavations have revealed several important shrines within the ancient city walls, including a temple to Caesar Augustus, a temple to Zeus, a small worship area for Nemesis, and even a temple to the "dancing goats". (Above) On the rock cliff above the spring are niches from the Roman period which once held statues dedicated to Pan. The beautiful Banias waterfall is less than a mile from the shrines of Pan (right).

Mount Tabor

"Thou hast created the north and the south, Tabor and Hermon sing for joy at your name." (Psalm 89:11)

Mount Tabor:
Basilica of the Transfiguration

Matthew 17:1-2 records that Jesus took three disciples "To a mountain alone and was transfigured, His face shining like the sun." Byzantine pilgrims thought Mt. Tabor matched the description in the Biblical passage, and built a church on this mountain top to commemorate the Transfiguration. Since then, most archaeologists have abandoned the idea, but the Basilica of the Transfiguration, built in 1924, is still a beautiful reminder of the story. The theme of the very impressive church is "things that are changed".

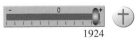

1924

Beth Shean / Scythopolis

Not far away, at the edge of Mt. Gilboa, the ruins of Beth Shean stand 80 feet above the surrounding plain. The body of King Saul was hung on the wall of this city after his armies were defeated by the Philistines (1 Samuel 28-31). Solomon later rebuilt the city's great walls.(1 Ki. 4).

By the third century BCE a magnificent Greek-style city emerged. The city's name was changed to Scythopolis to honor the mercenary soldiers that were imported from Scythia, near the Black Sea. The city lasted through the Roman, Byzantine and early Arab periods until its final destruction in 749 CE.

-1050

Mt. Gilboa

*T*he gospels tell us that while Jesus was on a journey in the area, He healed ten lepers along the road "between Samaria and Galilee" (Lk. 17).

Near the tree-lined road that follows the southern edge of the Jezreel Valley (right), is the beautiful natural pool at Sachne, popular with swimmers throughout the hot summer months (above).

Mt. Gilboa is a lush forest. Springs flow from its base, like that at Ein Harod, the site of the selection of Gideon's army (Judges 7).

Samaria

In the center of the country, the city of Samaria is surrounded by rolling hills covered with olive trees. King Omri built this city centuries before Jesus was born (876 BCE).

The remains of a round tower near the theatre of the ancient city (above), is all that is left of what was called in Hellenistic times "the finest monument" in the land. The Roman city had a colonnaded main street (left) for shopping.

Jesus is recorded to have passed through the greater territory of Samaria only twice (Jn 4:1ff; Lk. 9:51-56) during His ministry, as Jews normally "had no dealings with the Samaritans" (Jn. 4:9-10).

-876

Jacob's Well

In Nablus (Sychar), near Samaria, the Greek Orthodox maintain what many believe is Jacob's well.
Here, Jesus spoke to a woman saying, "...whoever drinks of the water I give him will never thirst." (John 4:13)

380

The Samaritans

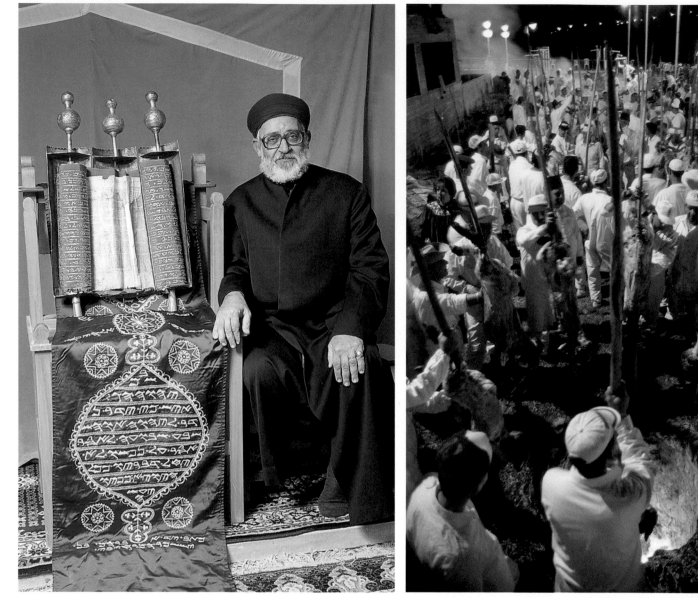

Numbering nearly one million at the time of Jesus, today there are only 600-700 Samaritans remaining in the Holy Land. About 300 live south of Nablus on top of Mount Gerizim (Jn. 4:20).

Though small in number, the Samaritans continue to practice their faith according to ancient custom. Their Torah scrolls (above) are hand copied in a script related to ancient Hebrew.

Each spring the Samaritans gather on Mount Gerizim for a 40-day "Passover" feast, including ritual sheep sacrifices.

Wadi Qelt

On a trip to Jerusalem late in His ministry, a scribe asked Jesus, "Who is my neighbor?" Jesus responded to the question with the story of the Good Samaritan (Lk. 10:30-37), set along Wadi Qelt, on a perilous desert road that connected ancient Jericho and Jerusalem. In the story, a man was beaten and left for dead by robbers. A kind Samaritan mercifully helped after the wounded man was passed by both a Temple priest and a Levite.

Today, along the old Roman road, visitors can view the Greek Orthodox monastery of St. George of Koziba. Founded in 420 CE by five hermits in a small cave, the monks eventually built a fifty-foot bell tower, a domed chapel, and an open courtyard for their private use. These buildings were completely destroyed in the Crusader Period, but rebuilt around 1900.

420

Ein Gedi

In contrast to the harsh desert in the wilderness of Judea, the canyon (also called a wadi) at Ein Gedi has a waterfall and flowing stream most of the year that keeps the area green and filled with wildlife. The nature reserve is filled with stunning views of the flora and fauna commonly mentioned in the Bible. Ein Gedi means "spring of the young goat" and is today the home of four large herds of ibex (wild mountain goats).

This wadi was where David hid from King Saul (1 Samuel 24). Later, the area was known for its medicinal and sweet smelling plants, (Song of Sol.1) date palms and desert aloes.

Wildlife in the Land

As a land bridge between the continents of Africa, Asia and Europe, millions of birds and a variety of species of animals migrating from these continents, thrive in the land, including gazelles, orynx (albinos), and ostriches.

South of Ein Gedi, a high plateau called Masada ("stronghold") was fortified about 100 BCE.

Masada was originally built by the Hasmonean ruler Alexander Jannaeus, then improved by Herod the Great, who built luxurious accommodations within its walls.

Seized by the Zealots in the revolt against Rome, Masada was the site of the mass suicide of 960 Jewish defenders who died rather than become slaves of the Romans in 73 CE. The caldarium, or hot bathing room, was discovered near the northern palace (above), along with utensils and even a pair of first century sandals.

The Dead Sea

The Dead Sea is the lowest accessible point on the earth. At 1300 feet below sea level, this unique sea has five to seven times the minerals of other seas, and is ten times saltier than Mediterranean.

The Southern Deserts

*T*he southern two-thirds of the land are desert, including the Biblical "Wilderness of Paran" (Num. 10) and "Wilderness of Zin" (Num. 27). Though the gospels are silent about travels here, the desert played a big part in the history of the Jewish people.

The stories of the Exodus (Ex. 1-40), and the journey of Elijah (1 Ki. 19) were the basis of Hebrew education from the time Jesus was a boy. Natural beauty in these deserts include springs (upper right), and formations like the "pillars of Amram" and "mushroom" at Timnah (below).

Eilat and The Red Sea

East of the Sinai peninsula, the Red Sea reaches into the valley of the Jordan- rift as far north as Eilat. A port city, this vibrant entertainment center is filled with modern new hotels, elegant yachts, and beautiful palm-lined beaches.

Sunny and warm throughout the year, Eilat is a traveller's paradise in the winter months. Eilat is the probable site for Ezion-geber of the Bible (1 Ki. 9:26), and even Solomon must have noted its natural beauty!

A protected reef just yards from the shore can be explored in a diver's wet-suit, or in the Coral World Underwater Observatory (p.76, lower), a popular attraction which draws hundreds of visitors every day.

The stark mountains and dry landscape around the gulf are starkly contrasted with the rich colors found beneath the sea. (right).

Jerusalem

Set in the mountainous terrain of Judea, Jerusalem was originally a Canaanite stronghold called Jebus until it was taken by King David's army about 1000 BCE. (2 Sam. 5). Solomon built and dedicated the "First Temple" there (1 Ki. 6).

The later kings of Judah ruled from the city and were buried there (2 Ki. 8:24). Jerusalem was eventually destroyed in 586 BCE by the Babylonians (Jer. 39). After a painful period of exile - reflected in some of the "sad songs" of the Psalmists (Ps.137), Jews were allowed to return under a decree of King Cyrus of Persia, and rebuild the destroyed Temple (Ezra 1). That Temple stood, much improved and enlarged by Herod the Great, until its destruction in 70 CE by the Romans.

For more than four thousand years the inhabitants of Jerusalem built their homes within fortress-like walls that were moved farther out as the population increased. In the 1860's, Moses Monifiore built a small settlement for the first pioneers to move beyond the old city walls. (below).

Today, Jerusalem is alive with cafes, resturants and shops both inside and outside the old city's walls. Alleyways were closed to traffic and paved in Jerusalem's golden stone, to provide both ambience, and a vast selection of oriental delicacies!

Holy places and shrines abound within the city's sixteenth century walls. The famous golden Dome of the Rock is the city's holiest Islamic site.

Nearby are more than fifty synagogues, several dozen churches, and about a dozen minarets. Weaving among the shrines are the thousands of people that live and work within the Medieval walls. Church bells are often heard throughout the city. In addition to the bells, Moslem calls to prayer cry out five times each day.

Jerusalem was a jewel sought after by conquerors like the Assyrians, Babylonians, Greeks, Romans, Byzantines, Arabs and Crusaders. With each successive conquest came alterations and adornments. Truly, as one historian has written, " The history of this city has been written in blood and stone."

1297

The land where the Church of the Holy Sepulchre was built was a cemetary during the time of Jesus, but before that functioned as a quarry dating back to the eighth century BCE. (above). The earliest church to recall the crucifixion and resurrection of Jesus was built on this location by Queen Helena in the fourth century CE.

Maps of the ancient city abound (left), and help historians and archaeologists locate many the various pilgrim sites from the differing periods.

The Gates of Jerusalem

Seven gates now lead into Jerusalem. Built by Sultan Sulieman the Magnificent in 1538-42 CE, they were a splendid golden gift to the city.

The Lion's Gate (upper left) which gets its name from the lions (above) on the face, is also called St. Stephen's Gate, because it is near the church that recalls the stoning of St. Stephen (Acts 7).

The Damascus Gate (above right) is the most ornate example of Ottoman architecture in the city.

The Zion Gate (right, upper) is scarred from two modern wars (1948 and 1967).

The Dung Gate (right, lower) was expanded by the British to allow for traffic (circa 1920).

Herod's Gate (left) fell to the Crusader conquest in 1099.

"Our feet are standing within thy gates, O Jerusalem that art built as a city that is compact together" (Ps. 122:2,3).

The beautiful Golden gate is closed now (right), guarded by a Moslem cemetery along the wall. It stands above the Susa Gate to the area know as "Solomon's porch" in the New Testament, the site of early Christian meetings (Acts 3:11).

The western gate is called Jaffa Gate (lower right) because it leads to the port town of Jaffa. Seen from above, the gate has the remains of a tower, one of those built by Herod the Great to protect his fortress.

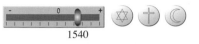

1540

Jerusalem

Palm Sunday and The Passion Week

With its long history of conquests and turbulent times, Jerusalem was the scene of the end of the teaching and healing "earthly ministry" of Jesus. He arrived at Bethany (p. 84) the Sabbath before the crucifixion (Jn. 12:1-12) and stayed there during the Passover week, walking each day through Bethpage (p. 85) into Jerusalem.

On Sunday, Jesus approached the village that marked the entry to Jerusalem (probably Bethpage), and sent two disciples to get a donkey for him to ride into the city (Mt. 21:1ff), recalling the prophecy of Zechariah 9:9, "Your king comes..lowly, and riding upon an ass."

When the crowds that were visiting Jerusalem for the Passover saw Jesus arriving, they began to strip the trees of their palm branches and cry, "Hosanna, Son of David!" (Mk. 11:7ff). The procession is remembered today at the start of Christian Holy Week, which recalls the events of the Passion.

Bethany: The Tomb of Lazarus

*J*esus visited Bethany several times, and stayed with one of His four friends there - Lazarus, Mary, Martha, and Simon the former leper.

1952

*T*he Church of Lazarus (top) recalls the most famous event at Bethany, the raising of Lazarus (Jn. 11). Built in 1952 above three older churches, the beautiful apse and altar (above) recollects the words of Jesus, "I am the resurrection and the life." Up the hill from the church, a small door reveals 20 steps to the traditional tomb of Lazarus.

Bethpage

On top of the Mount of Olives, Bethpage ("house of green figs") is probably the village from which Jesus made His way by donkey into Jerusalem on Palm Sunday (Mt. 21).
A small Greek chapel containing the Crusader "mounting stone of Christ" was built in 1883, and is the starting point of the modern annual procession of Palm Sunday.

1883

Paternoster and Dominus Flevit

On the Mount of Olives, several churches mark scenes from the ministry of Jesus. One chapel is called Paternoster (below), Latin for "Our Father". This convent recalls the lesson of Jesus on prayer (Mt. 6:10-13).

The cave beneath the altar (lower left) was part of the fourth century church, to mark the nearby Ascension of Jesus (Acts 1). Not far down the slope of the Kidron Valley is Dominus Flevit (left, and p. 87), or "Our Lord Wept," recalling the tears of Jesus (Lk. 19:41).

1875

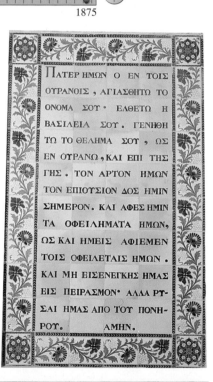

The Church of St. Mary Magdalene

*B*uilt between 1883-8, this classical Slavic style church of St. Mary Magdalene was commissioned by Czar Alexander III because Mary was the patroness saint of his family.

With seven onion-shaped spires, the church is maintained by the White Russian nuns. The church recalls Mary, who may have been the woman that anointed Jesus' feet with tears and ointment (Lk. 7) and "who loved much, because she was forgiven much."

1888

Kidron Valley Tombs

The "Pillar of Absalom" is actually a tomb from the first century CE, cut from bedrock to the cornice.

The traditional "Tomb of St. James" was the second century BCE burial for the priestly family of Hezir.

The pyramid-topped first century CE "Tomb of Zachariah" marks the opening of nearby catacombs.

The Mount of Olives Cemetery

Jesus stayed in Bethany during the Passover week (Mk. 11:11,19). Except for Palm Sunday," He travelled on foot every day to the city of Jerusalem. The road from Bethany passed north of the vast cemeteries along the ridge of the Mount of Olives. Pilgrims avoided coming close to the tombs, not wanting to defile themselves during the holy festival season.

This daily journey that Jesus and His disciples took was to the Temple that stood about where the golden Dome of the Rock stands today. During that Passover, these walks of Jesus back and forth to the Temple were the scenes for a number of important recorded sayings. Some included the cursing of the fig tree (Mt. 21:18ff; Mk. 11:13ff), and the Olivet Discourse (M 24:3-26:2).

Along the slope of the Mt. of Olives is the oldest continually used cemetery in the world. Graves dating back four thousand years rest beside modern ones. Many Biblical scholars relate this area to the "Vale of Jehosophat" (Joel 3:2), the place of final judgment.

The Tomb of Mary

*T*he traditional Tomb of the Virgin Mary is near Gethsemane at the bottom of the Mount of Olives. Pilgrims report that by the sixth century a church already stood on the site. Though the facade of the church (lower left) is probably from the 12th century CE, scholars believe the massive stairway (above) may either be a part of an earlier church (590 CE), or a Crusader structure (1130).

590

The markets of the Old City of Jerusalem reveal the time-honored trading customs of the Near East. The "shuk" is filled with the pungent smell of spices and resonant calls of street vendors.

This market boasts a fantastic variety of goods made in brass or ceramics, and a colorful cast of characters hawking their wares.

The Gihon Spring & Hezekiah's Tunnel

Located in the Kidron Valley (left), the Gihon spring was the ancient water supply for Jerusalem. King David's men conquered the city by crawling through the Jebusite water shaft (2 Sam. 5). Hundreds of years later, King Hezekiah helped defend the city from the Assyrians (2 Chr. 32) by diverting the water through a 512 meter tunnel and into a pool.

On a trip to Jerusalem, Jesus commanded a blind man to wash in the pool and be healed (John 9). Visitors can still walk through this water-filled tunnel (lower right) which ends at the famous Siloam Pool (lower left).

-700

The Cenacle

*T*he evening before His arrest, Jesus ate a meal with His disciples in a secluded place (Jn. 13). The "Last Supper" of Jesus is recalled in the Cenacle, or "dining room." Though this building is from a much later period it marks the location of an earlier structure which was probably in the Essene quarter on Mt. Zion. The Essenes celebrated some holidays earlier than the rest of the Jewish community.

So, if Jesus ate His meal among them, this could solve the riddle how He ate what appears to be a Passover lamb (Lk. 22:15), and yet was already on the cross by the time the lambs were slain in the Temple (Mt. 27:27ff). The establishment of the Eucharist or Communion, was part of that evening (Mk. 14, Lk 22). Years later Christians also began to recall the coming of the spirit (Acts 2) in the place.

After the time of Jesus, the Hagia Zion Church was erected on the site. Destroyed in 614 CE, the site was rebuilt in the 12th Century as an upper chapel (Cenacle) and lower chapel (dedicated to King David). The upper chapel became a mosque under the Turks, who added the prayer niche and beautiful windows, and incorporated older artistic pillars (right).

Mt. Zion

Mt. Zion originally referred to the area King David's city occupied, but a later tradition moved the name to this ridge (above). The mountain became part of the walled city of Jerusalem under Hezekiah's expansion (8th Century BCE).

Mt. Zion was entirely enclosed by the old city's walls during the New Testament period. Suliman the Magnificent's two architects rebuilt the walls in the sixteenth century, but were reportedly executed because they left Mt. Zion outside the ramparts.

The Tomb of David

(Above) *King David was buried in the City of David (1 Ki. 2:10) which probably refers to a nearby hill that contained his city. The tradition of his burial here was first mentioned by the traveller Benjamin of Tudela (1172 CE), who visted the site. The burial chamber stone is covered with an embroidered cloth of royal purple, adorned with crowns that once topped Torah scrolls, some saved from the Nazi Holocaust.*

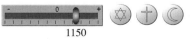

1150

(Left) *Also on Mt. Zion is the Church of the Dormition of Mary, built at the turn of the 20th century.*

The Garden of Gethsemane

After the "Last Supper," Jesus came to pray (Jn.18.)near an olive press in a grove called Gethsemane (literally, "the place of the press").

As Jesus prayed, His disciples fell asleep, only to be awakened by the sounds of the Temple guard led by Judas Iscariot. While Jesus was being placed under arrest, the disciples fled the garden.

30

Gethsemane: Church of the Agony

(Above) N*ear the bottom of the Mount of Olives is the "Church of the Agony" also called "The Church of All Nations." Built in 1924, its dramatic artwork recalls the betrayal by Judas (Jn. 18), and Jesus' agonizing prayer before His arrest.*

(Right) The altar is shaped like a cup, recalling the prayer of Jesus where He exclaimed, "Let this cup pass from Me" (Jn. 18). The mosaic above the altar shows Jesus in prayer.

1924

St. Peter en Gallicantu

After His arrest in the garden, the gospels record that Jesus was taken to Annas, and then to the High Priest Joseph Caiaphas (Jn. 18; Mk. 14). Peter and John followed Jesus into the High Priest's residence, where three times Peter denied knowing Jesus (Lk. 22)
St. Peter en Gallicantu or "St. Peter of the Cock Crowing" is built above the ruins of a palatial building thought by some to be Caiaphas' house. A main street (lower, p.101) from before the New Testament period was discovered nearby. The grey domed church was built by the Assumptionist Fathers in the 1950's on Mt. Zion's lower slope.

*W*hile digging the foundation of the church archaeologists discovered a mansion of at least 12 rooms. Amidst the building's ruins were a full set of weights and measures. This evidence added to the speculation that the home belonged to a former High Priest, the market official charged with checking weights in the scales. Rock cut caverns below the house (right) were used as stables. Some historians believe these were also used as prison cells for those who cheated in the market place.

If this were Caiaphas' house, Jesus may have been held in such a cell. (Mk. 14). Recent renovations of the churc have added a chapel dedicated to the denial and restoration of the Apostle Peter (above).

1951

The Pools of Bethesda

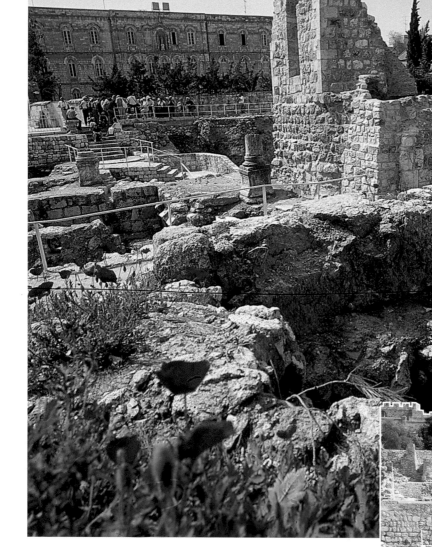

*J*esus visited Jerusalem many times before that fateful Passover season. He sometimes taught, sometimes healed. Some of His actions were frowned upon by the Temple leadership in the city. During one such incident when Jesus was on a visit to partake in a feast, He stopped at a pool one sabbath day and healed a man who had been crippled for 38 years. (Jn. 5).

The gospel describes the pool as having five porches. These pools were discovered by the White Fathers while excavating on the property of St. Anne's Church. The largest pool measured 350 feet long, 200 feet wide, and was about 40 feet deep. Colonnaded porches surrounded the pool and a large bridge (right) was built across the center.

The Church of St. Anne

About 1140 CE the Crusaders built the Church of St. Anne alongside the Bethesda pools, to recall the childhood home of the Virgin Mary.

According to an early church tradition, the parents of Mary - Joachim and Anne - lived north of the Temple Mount in a humble quarter of Jerusalem.

This is one of 35 churches built by the Crusaders. The sanctuary was used for a time by Salahadin as a Moslem seminary, and then abandoned.

It was restored 100 years ago, and still draws thousands of pilgrims a year. The acoustics are marvelous.

1140

The Via Dolorosa Stations I-IV

*E*ach Friday, the Franciscans lead a procession (below) along the "Stations of the Cross," a reflective pilgrim's walk that recalls the sufferings of Jesus in fourteen places of prayer.

*T*he Via Dolorosa or "Way of Sorrow" is the traditional path Jesus took on the fateful journey from His condemnation by Pontius Pilate (*Mt. 27:11-26; Lk. 23:13ff*) to the Crucifixion (*Jn. 19:17-30*) at Calvary. The route winds its way from the ruins of the ancient Antonio Fortress (above) to the Church of the Holy Sepulchre (pp. 110-117).

1850

The first devotional walks in Jerusalem were organized by the Franciscans back in the fourteenth century.

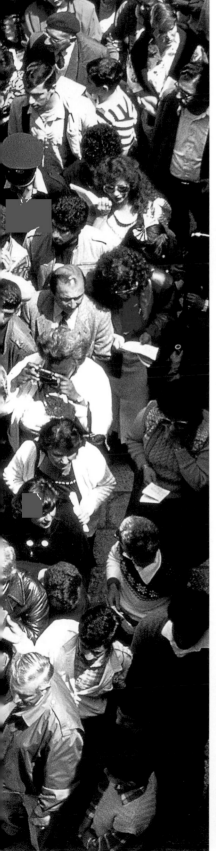

The Via Dolorosa starts in the courtyard of the Omariyeh school, once used by the Turks as army barracks. Across the street are two chapels recalling that under the governor Pilate, Jesus was tried, condemned, and beaten by Roman soldiers.

The "Chapel of the Flagellation" has powerful artwork of the bound Savior above the altar (below), within a dome crowned with thorns.

*W*ithin the same compound as the Chapel of the Flagellation at the beginning of the Via Dolorosa, the Chapel of the Condemnation recalls the sentence of Jesus by Pontius Pilate (Jn. 19:1-6). This chapel is also within the area of the ancient Antonio Fortress, a large barracks for Roman soldiers at the time of Jesus.

*T*he architect of the chapel combined painting and sculpture in the center apse (above) to capture the scene for pilgrims who visit the chapel today. Station I is "Jesus was Condemned". Station II is outisde the chapel where "Jesus recieved His Cross". Station III is a few hundred yards down the street, after the road turns to the south. It is a place to remember "Jesus fell the first time" (right).

*T*he sculpture of Thaddeus Zielinsky shows Jesus falling beneath the cross. It stands above the door to the Polish chapel. As pilgrims stop at Station III (center left), the marker placed along the road in 1947 by the Polish army, they read from Lamentations 1. Station IV, in front of the Armenian Catholic Chapel marks a reflection place for "Jesus was seen of His Mother", a place that reminds pilgrims of the pain experienced by Mary after the condemnation.

Ecce Homo

135

A small arch spans the Via Dolorosa between Stations II and III, (lower left) joining another arch in the apse of a chapel to the north (upper right). This is the "Ecce Homo" or "Behold the man!" chapel which belongs to the Convent of the Sisters of Zion (Jn. 19:5).

When eighteenth and nineteenth century explorers first identified the arches, they thought they were from the doorway of the Antonio Fortress, and were the place of Pilate's pronouncement. Scholars later decided the arches dated from the time of Hadrian (135 CE). The roof above the chapel offers an excellent view of the Via Dolorosa (above).

The Antonio Fortress

Herod rebuilt a Hasmonean palace between 37-35 BCE and renamed it the Antonia Fortress after his friend and mentor Marc Antony.

The heavy damage in the area caused by the fighting in 70 CE was repaired by Hadrian in 135 CE. Today the Sisters of Zion Convent marks the site. The model (above) shows the four huge towers of the original Antonia Fortress.

Cisterns were discovered (above) beneath a large pavement (center left). Scholars believe that Hadrian was responsible for closing the "Struthion pools" of the Antonia that were once open to the sky. On this pavement (left) are etchings characteristic of the "King's Game," where soldier played with the lives of condemned prisoners

-35

The Via Dolorosa Stations V-IX

Station V recalls Simon the Cyrene, who was compelled to carry the cross (above left). Station VI is the traditional site where "Veronica wiped the face of Jesus" (above center). At Station VII pilgrims reflect on the Savior's suffering as "Jesus fell the second time." Station VIII is marked by a small Latin Cross on the wall of a Greek monastery (below) where pilgrims remember that "Jesus consoled the daughters of Jerusalem".

A column near this door marks Station IX: "Jesus fell the third time".

The Church of the Holy Sepulchre

The Holy Sepulchre was perhaps the most important site for Christian pilgrimage from the Byzantine through the Crusader Periods. The building houses both the hill recalling Calvary, and the place of the tomb of the Resurrection of Jesus. The Gospel of St. John records that the body of Jesus was placed in a newly carved tomb originally meant for the wealthy Joseph of Arimathaea (Mt. 27:57-58). The gospel writer describes the tomb area as a place kept by a gardener (Jn. 20:15), not far from the place of the Crucifixion (cp. Mt. 27:57ff, Jn. 19: 41ff) with a rolling stone sealing the front of the tomb (see Mk. 16:3).

During the time of Jesus the city walls of Jerusalem did not extend as far north as they do today, and the site now inside the Church of the Holy Sepulchre was outside the north wall. In about the eighth century BCE the area had apparently been a stone quarry. By New Testament times, it was used as a cemetery.

The tombs were cut from bedrock, as was the local custom. Hadrian (135 CE) removed the tombs and built a temple to Zeus on the hill pilgrims call Golgotha, along with an altar to Venus at the place of the Sepulchre. These were both removed when Queen Helena built the first church here in 326 CE.

The Stations of the Cross of the Via Dolorosa continue within the Church of the Holy Sepulchre. Inside the main door (p. 111) is a flat stone that is often covered with flowers at Station XIII: "Jesus was taken down from the cross". At "the stone of anointing", tradition says that Jesus' body was anointed for burial (right).

On the terrace above the stone is Station X: "Jesus was stripped of His garments" (Mt. 27:35; Jn. 19:23).

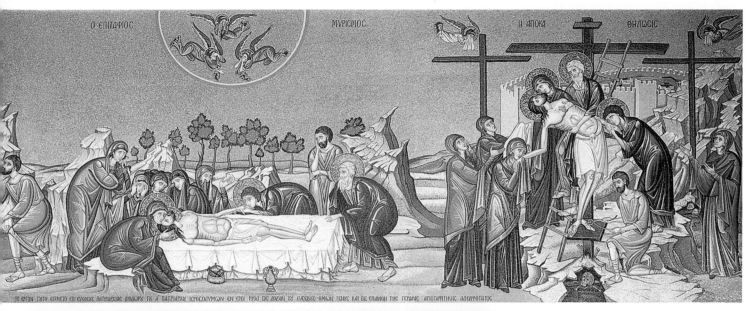

Station XI: "Jesus was nailed to the cross" (left), is represented in the mosaic on the wall of the chapel. At the Greek altar nearby is Station XII: "Jesus died on the cross" (p. 112, top).

Before reaching the Greek altar pilgrims pass by the little altar that recalls the heartbreak of Mary (above). Sculpted from wood in the sixteenth century, the artwork was sent from Lisbon and added to the church in 1778.

The end of the "Way of Sorrows" is at Station XIV: "Jesus was placed in the tomb" (p.115). The tomb that once stood in this location was completely removed long ago, probably by Hadrian in the erection of the altar to Venus.

When Queen Helena and Emperor Constantine built the first church to celebrate the Resurrection (326 CE), called the Anastasis ("Resurrection"), they constructed a round structure above the tomb location that has since been replaced.

The Anastasis was destroyed in the Persian raid of 614 CE, immediately rebuilt, and destroyed again by the Caliph Hakim in 1010. It was the condition of this shrine that became the central rallying cry for the European leaders organizing the Crusades. The tomb (above) today contains some portions of the original church, with many parts rebuilt by the Crusaders.
The interior of the tomb has an antechamber (left), and an inner chamber (above).

*T*here are six Christian communities that are involved in daily worship here: *The Greek Orthodox, Armenian, Latin (Roman) Catholic, Syrian Orthodox, Coptic and Ethiopian Churches.*

Gordon's Calvary

Next to the Garden Tomb is a rocky cliff that resembles a skull's face - with caves marking the eyes, nose and mouth. British General Gordon thought this was "Golgotha" or the place of the skull (Jn. 19:17), where Jesus' crucifixion took place. The discovery of a nearby tomb further supported Gordon's identification.

1883

The Garden Tomb

*F*ollowing General Gordon's statement that the tomb of the
Resurrection may be on the the hill he called "Golgotha,"
the Garden Tomb became a popular place to visit.

*Evidence of large water cisterns and a wine press aided in
identifying this site (cp. Jn. 19:41ff; Jn. 20:1ff).*

1883

Emmaus

1890

*T*he gospels and the Book of Acts record that the resurrected Jesus appeared to his followers on at least eleven occasions. One such appearance was to some travellers on the road to Emmaus (Lk. 24). The lovely Trappist Monastery at Latroun (top) is built on a hillside between Jerusalem and Tel Aviv near excavations (center; right) searching for the possible site of Emmaus.

The Ascension

Acts 1 records that Jesus took His disciples to the Mount of Olives, a Sabbath day's journey from Jerusalem, blessed and commissioned them, and then ascended into Heaven. Now called the Paternoster Church, Queen Helena used the location in the fourth century CE to build the earliest church recalling the Ascension (see p. 86).

Fifty years later a second church was erected, called the "Chapel of the Ascension," which later became a mosque (above).Yet another traditional site is at the Russian Church of the Ascension (left) whose tower has marked the skyline of Jerusalem since it was built in 1878.

The Dome of the Rock

*T*he third holiest site in the world to Islam is the Dome of the Rock, also called "the jewel of Jerusalem architecture".

Muslims call the plaza "Haram esh Sharif" or the "Noble Sanctuary,"and have revered the site since the Caliph Omar came into the area in 638 C.E.

The Arabic calligraphy band on the building.

The golden dome was recently recovered with an aluminum-gold alloy, donated by King Hussein of Jordan. The exterior ceramic tiles are modern (1963), but many of the interior mosaics are original (right).

A cabinet within the building houses what many Moslems say is a hair from the prophet Mohammed's beard. (right), a popular spot to make a wish. Another tradition suggests this is the mountain of "Jehovah Jireh" (Gen. 22:14), where Abraham nearly sacrificed Issac.

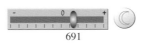

691

*B*uilt between 688-691 by Abd al Malik, the Ummayad ruler, this octagonal building measures 63 feet on each side, and is 180 feet tall. The dome is positioned over bedrock that may have been part of the threshing floor of Aruna (right), which King David purchased for the building of the ancient Temple (2 Sam 24).

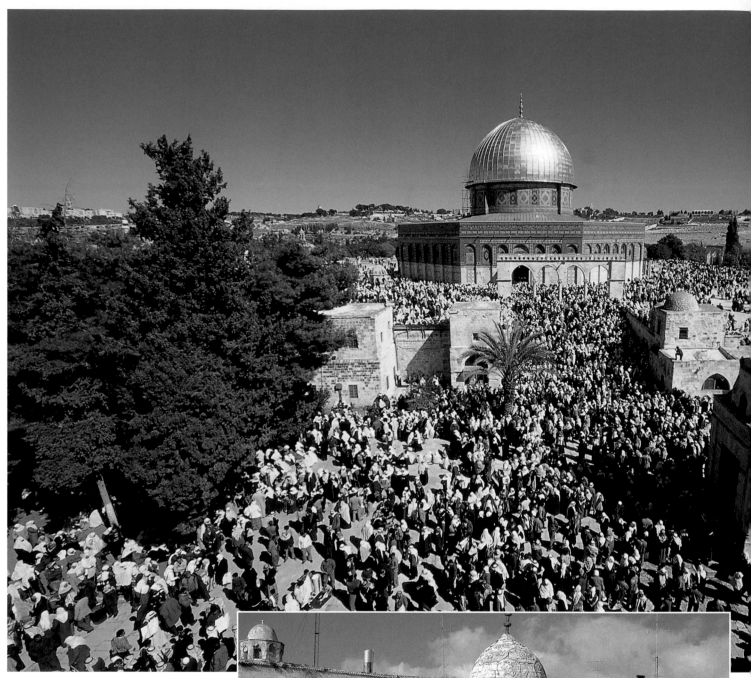

At prayer time during the Moslem festivals, the area around the Dome of the Rock is filled with worshippers. The plaza was originally levelled by Herod the Great to serve his magnificent Temple. Today, Moslems gather in the courtyard to hear the messages broadcast by loudspeakers from the Al Aqsa mosque. Exquisite examples of Near Eastern architecture (right) can be seen in the plaza, like the Qaytbay Sabil, a fountain dedicated in 1482.

Al Aqsa Mosque

The Al Aqsa Mosque (above) was built by Caliph el Walid in 705-714 CE. The structure was destroyed twice by severe earthquakes, and last rebuilt about 1040 CE. For 88 years Crusader knights used the area as a garrison. When Salahadin reclaimed the mosque for Islam in 1187, he added a prayer niche (mihrab), along with an elaborately carved wooden pulpit.(The pulpit was burned in 1969 by a crazed Christian tourist.) Renovations in 1938-42 included some interior marble columns donated by Benito Mussolini, and coffered ceilings from King Farouk of Egypt.

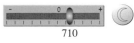

710

(Above) *The El Kas fountain was built during the same period as the nearby mosque. Here the traditional Moslem ritual of cleansing before prayer is practiced. Head, hands and feet are washed before the faithful bow to pray.*

(Left) *This large underground plaza is beneath the Al Aqsa mosque. No excavations of the site have been conducted, but some of the pillars appear to date back to the time of Herod the Great. The space was probably used as a stable by the Crusaders, when it received the traditional name "Solomon's stables".*

(Above) *The black and white designs with red accents found in different porch decorations are classic examples of Mameluke (1250-1517 CE) architecture. Similar designs dating from the same period can also be seen in Egypt.*

The Mamelukes overthrew the dynasty of Salahadin in 1250 CE., then began a series of successful campaigns that lead to the expulsion of the Crusader army at Acco.

This victory ended the last Crusader hold on the land. But the Mamelukes reign was filled with in-fighting, which made it difficult to beautify the city of Jerusalem. Some exceptions can be found in the Haram area. (left, above)

(Left, below) While Europe plunged into the "Dark Ages," Islam proudly carried on artisan traditions, knowledge of the healing arts (apothecaries), and classical geometric architecture. Beautiful examples of these contributions can be seen within the Al Aqsa Mosque.

The Tower of David

Even in drawings one hundred years old, (below) the tower beside the Jaffa Gate was one of Jerusalem's landmarks.

Scholars report that Herod the Great built a large tower here and named it after his brother, Phasael.

The tower was destroyed by the Romans in 70 C.E., but the base of the tower remained. By the seventeenth century, a minaret was added to call Moslems to prayer five times each day.

-30

Jerusalem: The Jewish Quarter

Heavily destroyed between 1949 and 1967, the Jewish Quarter came to life again after the Six Day War (June, 1967). During its reconstruction, parts of ancient Jerusalem surfaced for the first time in thousands of years.

The Cardo, a major thoroughfare during the Byzantine era, was discovered with its colonnade (above left). Homes destroyed by the Romans were also unearthed (below left). Most of the quarter was restored, but one synagogue (below), called Hurva "the ruin," reminds visitors of the destruction that befell the quarter.

The Knesset

The Knesset houses the 120 representatives of the Parliament that draft legislation for the country, the only democracy in the middle east. Built with money from the family of James de Rothschild, the building cost more than 7 million dollars, and also contains a national library of over 55,000 volumes. The menorah, or seven branched candleabra, was a gift of the British Parliament.

1966

Yad Vashem

The Holocaust memorial of Yad Vashem includes a historical museum, the valley of lost communities, a sculpture garden, the exhibit in memory of the millions of murdered children, and somber halls that recall the horrors of the Nazi regime. The Hall of Remembrance (lower left) or "Ohel Yizkor" is where memorial services are held. The room contains an eternal flame, as well as the names of Nazi death camps. At the entrance to the children's memorial (below) is a statue of orphans being held by Dr. Janusz Korczak the polish Jewish educator who valiantly tried to save them.

The People of the Land

The beauty and diversity of this land is evident in its people and its landscape. The ancient is blended with the modern. The native Israeli is called a "sabra" (above), named for the prickly pear cactus - sweet inside but protected by sharp thorns.

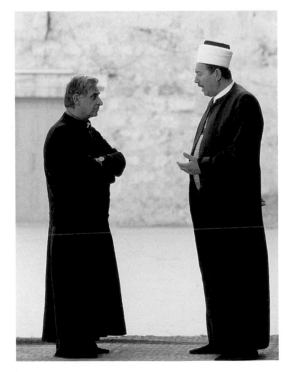

Tel Aviv

Tel Aviv, founded in 1909, means "mound of spring." This modern city grew out of the ancient port of Jaffa (Joppa - 2 Chr. 2:16; Jonah 2:3).

Though the original settlement was quite modest, today the greater Tel Aviv area boasts more than one million people.

Tel Aviv is the economic hub of modern Israel, with an array of cultural festivals, museums and exhibits. Built along the beautiful Mediterranean shoreline, there is a marina, a long beautiful beach, and plenty of restaurants and shops.

1909

Caesarea

Halfway between Tel Aviv and Haifa along the Mediterranean coastline are the ruins of ancient Caesarea. Built in 20 BCE by Herod the Great, the city was once a world class port. For nearly 600 years Caesarea was the official capital of what the Romans called "Provincia Judea."

During the time of Jesus, Pontius Pilate ruled from this city in the name of Rome. Philip the Deacon ministered here (Acts 8:40), and Peter preached to the Centurion Cornelius (Acts 10) in the city. Paul was imprisoned here (Acts 26).

Pieces of once beautiful statues, like the foot above show that the city contained much art work from the Roman period.

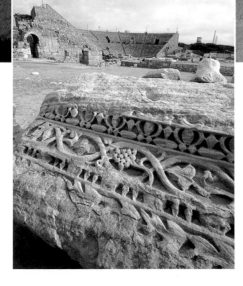

*E*xtensive excavations have revealed a large theatre on the southern edge of the city (p. 136, upper), a Crusader moat and wall built in 1101 C.E. (p. 136, lower), and a water aqueduct (above).

The Hashemite Kingdom of Jordan

Jerash

Jerash, or ancient Gerasa, is a well restored ruin about 24 miles north (40 km.) of Amman, along the Biblical "King's Highway." The city was populated from about 3000 BCE, but reached its peak when the Seleucids built a new city after defeating the Ptolemies. After a short occupation by Alexander Janneus, Rome made the city part of the Decapolis.

Zealots took Jerash during the first revolt, but it was quickly recaptured by Vespasian. The city prospered in Byzantine times. Jerash came under Arab rule about 630 CE, and has been Moslem ever since. The local mosque (left) is still the pride of this community.

Excavations that began in the 1920's uncovered a large Forum of the Roman city (p. 138, top), and the cardo, a street lined (above) with more than 250 doric and ionic columns.

Stone work on the site shows exquisite craftsmanship. The worn tracks made by chariots' wheels are still seen in the streets (above). One tradition suggests that St. Paul spent time in the city after leaving Damascus (Gal. 1:17-18). The term "Arabia" in the text may have referred to the desert trade route between cities, rather than to the Arabian peninsula.

-160

Mt. Nebo

*T*he exact location of the Mt. Nebo of the Bible is uncertain (cp. Num. 23) but using Christian tradition as a guide, a church commemorating the site was built in the fourth century on a rocky escarpment six miles north of Madaba. (Top) The mountain from which Moses viewed the promised land (Dt. 32-34) was originally recalled by a small chapel. By the sixth century that chapel had become a large monastery.

*A*rchaeologists of the Franciscan Biblical Institute discovered a large and colorful mosaic floor (above, center) in what was probably the main sanctuary of the monastery. The Franciscans have maintained the property for visitors since the early 1930's.

Madaba

By the sixth century, Madaba had a large church with an elegant mosaic floor (left) that contained a detailed map of the nearby holy places.

The map of Jerusalem (above) has been used extensively by historians to locate sites in the city including the Hagia Zion Church, the Nea Church, and the Cardo (main street) of the city.

550

*M*adaba is a city along the "King's Highway," the important north-south route through Transjordan. The first Biblical reference to Madaba is in the story of the Israelites' battles with the Amorite King Sihon (Num. 21). Later the city was conquered by David (1 Chr. 19). Madaba is mentioned in King Mesha's stele, the famous "Moabite Stone." Mattathias' son John was killed at Madaba (1 Macc. 9) during the revolt of the Maccabees. According to the historian Josephus, the Nabateans received the city from the Hasmoneans as a reward for their alliance during the revolt.

Petra

The Nabatean's "Rose Red City" of Petra is made up of buildings cut out of the rock in a southern Jordan canyon. Historians first noticed the Nabateans around the sixth century BCE. Originally they were traders that developed routes across the deserts, transporting goods from the east including spices and perfumes.

They established forts, then cities, to protect these profitable routes, and eventually were more involved in maintaining the routes than in the trade itself.
An ingenious people, they also developed very advanced irrigation techniques for their crops.

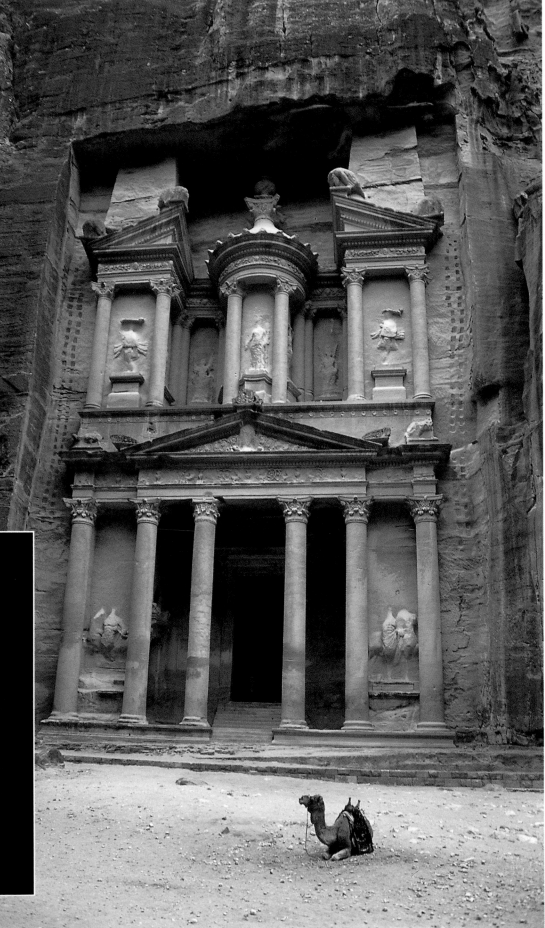

*P*etra is located in a canyon that provids excellent natural security (p. 142 lower). In 312 BCE, the city successfully defended itself against several attacks by the Greeks. Even in 63 BCE the Roman General Pompey could not take the city. Trajan finally defeated the Nabatean armies elsewhere, and they subsequently forfeited the city to Rome in 106 CE.

*B*y the Byzantine period, the Nabateans had lost their power, and Petra most of its population. A small group of Christians converted some of the larger Nabatean tombs into church meeting places. Gradually, the city was abandoned.

The former beauty of the city and its once thriving culture is evident in the large theater (left) and its elegant treasury building (above). Though the Nabateans built cities on a Greek plan and style, interior etchings and small details in the cornice work reflect a distinct and unique culture.

-300

2000 **+**

1500

1000

500

0

-500

-1000

-1500

-2000

-7000

−

ISRAEL 1948 CE

Turkish Ottoman Period 1517-1918 CE
The Ottomans defeated the Mamelukes and took Constantinople and Egypt. Sultan Suliman rebuilt the walls of Jerusalem. A series of 'pashas' follow with no desire to rebuild or improve Jerusalem.

Mameluke Period 1250-1517 CE
The Bahri Mamelukes overpowered the ruling Arab dynasty, and struggled from their bases in Egypt to hold off the Syrian Mongols. The land became an important supply line.

Crusader Period 1099-1250 CE
Pope Urban II called for the liberation of Christian Holy sites. After taking Jerusalem, the Moslem population was massacred. Baldwin I established the monarchy of Latin kingdom. After Saladin was victorious at Hattin, the Crusaders gained some access to holy sites by treaty.

Early Arab Period 640-1099 CE
Muhammad's armies seized a weakened Roman empire at Yarmuk. The Ummayad, Abassid and Fatmid dynasties built. Many churches were destroyed and the Turks blocked Christian pilgrimages to the Holy land.

Byzantine Period 324-640 CE
Constantine moved Roman Capital to Byzantium (Contstantinople). Christianity becomes the official state religion. The church grows rapidly. There are two destructive attacks - the Samaritan Revolt (529) and Persian attack (614).

Roman Period 63 BCE-324 CE
Pompey took Jerusalem. Rome used the land as buffer with the Parthian Empire. Herod the Great led the province with firm loyalty to Rome. The second Temple was built. Herod's son lacked his father's ability to rule. Rome ruled with a heavy hand. The Jews revolted and Titus destroyed the Temple and upper Jerusalem. Jews again revolted under Bar Kochba. Hadrian destroyed Jerusalem and renamed the city Aelia Capitolina. The land became the backwash of the empire. The Jews migrated to the Galilee.

Hellenistic Period 332-63 BCE
Alexander the Great conquered Persia introducing Hellenism as a major factor in world culture. After his death the Ptolemies held Egypt and Israel, and the Seleucids held Syria and Babylon. The Seleucids defeated the Ptolemies and seized the Jewish Priesthood. The Maccabean revolt followed. Jewish rule was developed and the kingdom was restored to an extent not seen since the days of David and Solomon.

Persian Period 538-332 BCE
After the Babylonian captivity some Jews were allowed by Cyrus (who had conquered Babylon a year before), to return to Judah. Nehemiah became the Governor / rebuilder, and Ezra re-established the Temple system under loose independence.

Iron Ages 1200-586 BCE
Israelites settled in the hill country and the Philistines settled along the southern plains coast. Judges ruled until pressure from Israel's enemies made a monarchy more appealing to the people. Saul became Israel's first king. David expanded empire and Solomon consolidated it. Kingdom is divided following Solomon's death. Later Assyria conquered Israel and Babylon conquered Judah, destroying Jerusalem and the Temple.

Bronze Ages 2800-1200 BCE
Copper and Tin was mixed to produce Bronze for heavier weaponry. The Chariot was developed. Empires arose in Egypt (who controlled the coastal highways) and Mesopotamia (who developed a trade route in the fertile crescent). Canaanite city states thrive. The decedents of Abraham were sold into slavery in Egypt. Moses led people from Egypt, and the Israelites took land of Canaan. (Gen. 12-50)

Copper Ages 4000-2800 BCE
Copper was the major material used for weapons.
The potter's wheel was in use. Fortified towns and commerce routes in many areas.

Prehistory: Stone Age
Before 4000 BCE Skeletons of humans and large animals found. The abundance of flint in the area attracted Nomads. Jericho appeared as a city state in the Jordan Valley at around 7000 BCE.